CARRY ON MY HUNGRY SON COOKBOOK COPY

A Deliciously Supernatural Cookbook

Fantastey Inc

CONTENTS

CHAPTER ONE

SO GET THIS...

This cookbook was crafted as an homage, each page
serving as a culinary journey inspired by the lives of Sam

and Dean Winchester. Within these recipes are embedded the secrets and wisdom gleaned from their years of confronting supernatural threats from both Hell and Earth (and occasionally, the divine). While the epic tales of the Winchester brothers are so vast they inspired God himself to write volumes about them, under the pen name Carver Edlund, this book honors them by highlighting one of the Winchester brothers' greatest loves in the world: food.

Food has always been an instrumental part of the hunter's journey. It offers far more than just nourishment. A well-prepared meal can be a source of self-soothing, a nice reward after a long day's work, a way for one to connect with their past by evoking memories of moments long forgotten, and, of course, a meal can offer immersible comfort. Ultimately, food is a source of strength for hunters physically, emotionally, and mentally.

What's more, when a new hunter requests guidance about their famous predecessors or is eager to know what dangers may arise in the battles ahead, the information they desire is often unveiled over satisfying meals enjoyed together.

It is our great pleasure to share with you some of the most iconic culinary preferences of legendary hunters, demons, angels, and the like. These recipes come from the actual show information. Their tastes and experiences are now collected in the Winchester journals for others to peruse and learn from. The wayward sons, Sam and Dean, have laid their heavy heads to rest, and boy, do they deserve it. But their story will continue to live on in the meals enjoyed by them, their family, friends, and even their enemies.

So, grab your apron, prepare your ingredients, and delve into a SUPERNATURAL world of flavors.

CHAPTER TWO

SEASIDE SHACK BACON BURGER WITH CHEESE

In the episode Lucifer Rising, Zachariah reveals to Dean that the angels actually want the apocalypse to happen. According to their angelic belief, this event would lead to paradise on Earth after the defeat of evil. However, Lucifer must be set free for this to occur, and the subsequent battles must take place. He attempts to placate Dean with an offer of Dean's favorite burgers and fries from the Seaside Shack.

Serving Size: 4 burgers

Time: Approximately 30 minutes

Ingredients:

For the Burger Patties:

- 1 lb. (450g) ground beef (80% lean)

- 1/4 cup breadcrumbs

- 1 garlic clove, minced

- 1/4 cup finely chopped onion

- 1/2 tsp salt

- 1/2 lb. (225g) ground pork

- 1/4 tsp black pepper

- 4 hamburger buns

For the Toppings:

- 8 slices of bacon

- Sliced tomatoes

- 4 slices of your favorite cheese (e.g., American, cheddar)

- Lettuce leaves

- Sliced pickles

- Mustard and ketchup (optional)

Materials:

- Grill or stovetop griddle

- Mixing bowl

- Frying pan

- Tongs

- Serving platter

Instructions:

1. Begin by heating your grill or stovetop griddle to medium-high heat.

2. In a mixing bowl, combine ground beef, ground pork, breadcrumbs, chopped onions, minced garlic, salt, and black pepper. Thoroughly mix the ingredients until well blended, then shape the mixture into four equal-sized burger patties.

3. In a skillet over medium heat, cook the bacon slices until they become crispy. Once done, place them on paper towels to remove excess grease.

4. Set the burger patties on the preheated grill or griddle and cook for about 4-5 minutes per side or until they reach your preferred level of doneness. During the last minute of cooking, add a slice of cheese to each patty and allow it to melt.

5. While the burgers cook, you can toast the hamburger buns on the grill or in the skillet until they turn lightly brown.

6. On the bottom half of each toasted bun, place a leaf of lettuce. Top with a cooked burger patty that has melted cheese. Add two crispy bacon slices, slices of tomato, and pickle slices.

7. If you like, add ketchup and mustard to the top half of the buns.

8. Finish your burger by placing the top bun on the assembled ingredients.

9. Transfer your Seaside Shack Bacon Burger With Cheese to a serving platter and savor it with your favorite side dishes. Enjoy!

Chef's Tips:

- Get creative with your burger toppings! You can add sautéed mushrooms, caramelized onions, or avocado slices for extra flavor and texture.

- If you prefer a different type of cheese, feel free to use your favorite. Blue cheese, Swiss, and pepper jack are all excellent choices.

- Serve the burgers with a side of coleslaw, french fries, or a fresh salad for a complete meal.

CHAPTER THREE

DEAN'S BREAKFAST EGG BURGER

Dean eats a breakfast egg burger entitled "Baby." This episode is unique and fan-favorite thanks to its unique narrative style since the entire episode is shown from the perspective of the Impala, affectionately named "Baby" by Dean. In this episode, Dean is seen enjoying a breakfast egg burger during a scene where he and Sam are having a meal in the Impala. Dean is clearly a man who would eat burgers for every meal for the rest of his life if he could.

Serving Size: 1 burger

Time: Approximately 15-20 minutes

Ingredients:

- 1 hamburger bun

- 1/2 lb. (225g) ground breakfast sausage (pork or turkey)

- 1 large egg

- 1 slice of American cheese

- 1 teaspoon butter

- Black pepper & salt, to taste

- 2 slices of bacon

- Optional: Ketchup, hot sauce, or other condiments of your choice

Materials:

- Frying pan

- Small saucepan (for cooking bacon)

- Spatula

- Cooking ring (optional, for a perfectly round egg)

- Toaster (for toasting the bun)

Instructions:

1. In a small saucepan, cook the bacon slices until they are crispy. Once done, place them on paper towels to drain excess grease.

2. If you have a cooking ring, place it in the frying pan, then melt the butter inside it. This helps shape the egg. Crack an egg into the ring and cook it to your preferred level of doneness (e.g., sunny-side up or over-easy). You can carefully shape the egg with a spatula if you don't have a ring.

3. While the egg is cooking, form the ground breakfast sausage into a patty slightly larger than the hamburger bun. Season it with salt and black pepper. Cook the sausage patty in the same pan until it's browned and cooked through.

4. Toast the hamburger bun until it has lightly browned. Place the cooked sausage patty on the bottom bun, then add a slice of American cheese. Next, add the cooked bacon and the fried egg on top.

5. If desired, add ketchup, hot sauce, or your preferred condiments to the top bun.

6. Place the top bun on the assembled ingredients to complete your breakfast egg burger.

Chef's Tips:

- Boost the nutritional value of your breakfast burger by adding some sautéed spinach. It adds a nice pop of color and adds more nutrients to your meal.

- For a spicy kick, consider adding a dash of hot sauce or a slice of jalapeño.

- Serve this hearty breakfast burger with a side of hash browns or crispy tater tots for the full "Supernatural" experience.

CHAPTER FOUR

FREAKIN' WORTH IT SPICED APPLE PIE TOPPED WITH VANILLA RUM ICE CREAM

Dean, portrayed as a rugged, tough, and often stoic character, has a soft spot for classic American comfort food, especially pie. Apple pie, throughout the series, becomes symbolic of Dean's yearning for a normal life and the simple, homely comforts that he rarely gets to enjoy due to his life as a hunter. Throughout the show, Dean mentions his love of apple pie far more than the audience ever sees him actually sit down and enjoy it. (It's become somewhat of a running joke amongst fans) Thankfully, although rare, there are times when we see him bite into a big, delicious slice of warm apple pie. And we're sure that it's freakin' worth it every time.

Serving Size: 8 slices

Time: Approximately 2 hours (including baking and cooling time)

Ingredients:

For the Spiced Apple Pie Filling:

- 6 cups of peeled, cored, and sliced apples (such as Granny Smith or Honeycrisp)

- 1/4 tsp ground nutmeg

- 2 tbsp all-purpose flour

- 1 tsp ground cinnamon

- 1/2 cup granulated sugar

- 1/4 tsp salt

- 1/4 cup brown sugar

- 1 tsp vanilla extract

- 1 tbsp lemon juice

- 1/4 tsp ground cloves

For the Pie Crust:
- 2 store-bought or homemade pie crusts (one for the bottom, one for the top)

For the Vanilla Rum Ice Cream:
- 2 tbsp dark rum (adjust to taste)

- 1 quart (4 cups) vanilla ice cream

Materials:

- 9-inch pie dish

- Mixing bowls

- Rolling pin

- Ice cream maker (if making homemade ice cream)

- Plastic wrap

- Foil

- Baking sheet

Instructions:

1. Preheat your oven to 425°F (220°C).

2. In a large mixing bowl, add your sliced apples, granulated sugar, brown sugar, flour, cinnamon, nutmeg, cloves, salt, lemon juice, and vanilla extract. Toss the apples until they are thoroughly coated with the mixture.

3. Roll out one of the pie crusts and gently place it into the pie dish, trimming any excess dough.

4. Pour the well-seasoned apple mixture into the prepared pie crust.

5. Roll out the second pie crust and position it over the apples. Seal the edges of the two crusts together by crimping with a fork or your fingers. Create a few slits in the top crust to allow steam to escape.

6. Cover the pie's edges with foil to prevent excessive browning.

7. Bake in your preheated oven for 45-55 minutes or until the crust becomes a beautiful golden brown and the filling starts to bubble.

8. Take the pie out of the oven and let it cool for at least 2 hours before serving.

9. If you're preparing homemade vanilla rum ice cream, follow the ice cream maker's instructions to combine vanilla ice cream and dark rum. After churning, transfer the ice cream into a lidded container and freeze until it reaches the desired firmness.

10. Cut a generous slice of the spiced apple pie and serve it with a scoop of homemade vanilla rum ice cream. Enjoy!

Chef's Tips:

- You can enhance the pie's flavor by adding a handful of raisins or chopped pecans to the apple filling.

- If you prefer a non-alcoholic version of the ice cream, you can skip the rum and enjoy classic vanilla ice cream.

- Feel free to drizzle caramel sauce or a warm spiced apple compote over the ice cream for an extra touch of sweetness and flavor.

CHAPTER FIVE

THE "BEST BANANA PANCAKES"

"Cus' Best Banana Pancakes" are mentioned in "Supernatural," specifically in the episode titled "Free To Be You and Me." In this episode, Sam Winchester, who is trying his best to live a normal life and avoid hunting, works as a bartender. The bar owner, Cus, is known for making the best banana pancakes. While you may not have the honor of knowing the chef of the "best banana pancakes" personally, you can still whip an amazing batch in your own home!

Serving Size: Approximately 4 servings

Time: Approximately 30 minutes

Ingredients:

For the Banana Pancakes:

- 2 ripe bananas, mashed

- 1 1/2 cups all-purpose flour

- 1 tsp baking powder

- 1/4 cup granulated sugar

- Cooking oil or additional butter for cooking

- 1/4 tsp salt

- 1 cup buttermilk

- 2 large eggs

- 1 tsp vanilla extract

- 2 tbsp unsalted butter, melted

- 1/2 tsp baking soda

For the Salted Caramel Sauce:
- 1 cup granulated sugar

- 1/2 tsp sea salt (adjust to taste)

- 1/2 cup heavy cream

- 2 tbsp unsalted butter

- 1/4 cup water

Materials:
- Mixing bowls

- Whisk

- Frying pan or griddle

- Spatula

- Small saucepan (for the caramel sauce)

Instructions:

1. In a mixing bowl, whisk together mashed ba-

nanas, buttermilk, eggs, melted butter, and vanilla extract.

2. In another bowl, combine flour, sugar, baking powder, baking soda, and a pinch of salt.

3. Pour the wet ingredients into the dry ingredients and stir until just mixed. It's okay if there are a few lumps; don't overmix.

4. Heat a frying pan or griddle over medium-high heat and lightly grease it with cooking oil or butter.

5. Pour about 1/4 cup of pancake batter onto the hot griddle for each pancake. Cook the pancakes until bubbles appear on the surface, then flip and cook until the other side turns a golden brown.

6. Repeat until you've used all the batter, and keep the cooked pancakes warm in a low oven at around 200°F (95°C) while you make the caramel sauce.

7. In a small saucepan, mix granulated sugar and water. Heat over medium heat, swirling the pan from time to time. Cook until the sugar dissolves

and the mixture turns a deep amber color.

8. Remove the saucepan from the heat, and gently stir in the heavy cream. Be careful, as it may bubble up.

9. Stir in unsalted butter and a pinch of sea salt. Taste and adjust the salt level to your liking.

10. Drizzle the warm salted caramel sauce over the banana pancakes. Enjoy!

Chef's Tips:

- You can add chopped nuts (such as walnuts or pecans) or chocolate chips to the banana pancake batter for extra texture and flavor.

- Top your banana pancakes with additional sliced bananas, whipped cream, or a scoop of vanilla ice cream for a decadent treat.

- To keep the pancakes warm while you make the caramel sauce, place them on a baking sheet in a low oven. This ensures they're all ready to serve at once.

CHAPTER SIX

EGG-WHITE OMELETS

In the episode "There's No Place Like Home," the brothers are in their usual spot - the bunker. Sam is talking to Cas on the phone, when Dean enters the room with egg-white omelets he made for himself and his little bro.

He must eat healthier if he wants to have any chance of controlling the Mark of Cain; this includes no drinking (if that's even possible for him) and 8 hours of rest daily, too.

Serving Size: 2 omelets

Time: Approximately 10-15 minutes

Ingredients:

- 1/4 cup diced bell peppers (any color)

- 6 large egg whites

- 1/4 cup diced onions

- Salt and pepper, to taste

- 1/4 cup diced tomatoes

- Cooking spray or a small amount of cooking oil

- 1/4 cup diced mushrooms

- 1/4 cup shredded cheese (cheddar, Swiss, or your choice)

- 1/4 cup diced ham or cooked turkey bacon (optional)

Materials:

- Non-stick frying pan

- Whisk

- Spatula

Instructions:

1. Take a bowl and put in the diced bell peppers, onions, tomatoes, mushrooms, and ham if you like. You can make it your own by adding your favorite veggies or protein.

2. Use another bowl to whip the egg whites until they get a bit frothy. Add a pinch of salt and pepper for some flavor.

3. Heat a non-stick frying pan over medium-high heat. Lightly spray it with cooking spray or use a small amount of oil.

4. Put the prepared filling into the pan and sauté it until the veggies are soft and the ham (if you're using it) gets a light golden color. Take the filling out of the pan and set it aside.

5. Reheat the pan and add some cooking spray or a touch of oil if needed.

6. Pour half of the beaten egg whites into the pan.

Tilt the pan to spread the egg whites evenly.

7. Cook for about 1-2 minutes or until the edges are firm and the middle is slightly runny.

8. Put half of the cooked vegetable and ham mix on one side of the egg white "pancake."

9. Carefully fold the other half of the omelet over the filling to make a half-moon shape. Cook for another minute until the omelet sets and takes on a light brown color.

10. Sprinkle half of the shredded cheese on top of the omelet.

11. Carefully slide the omelet onto a plate. Repeat the process to make the second omelet. Enjoy your meal!

Chef's Tips:

- You can customize the omelets by adding your favorite herbs or spices, such as chives, parsley, or a pinch of cayenne pepper.

- For a healthier option, use turkey bacon or skip the meat altogether.

- Serve your omelets with a side of fresh fruit, toast, or a small salad for a complete and balanced breakfast.

Chapter Seven

CHILI CHEESE FRIES

In the episode called "Tall Tales," Dean eats chili cheese fries. The brothers are investigating a series of bizarre and humorous events on a college campus that are eventually attributed to a Trickster. During the episode, Dean's love for food is portrayed in an over-the-top manner. He eats enormous portions of food, including a heaping plate of chili cheese fries, much to Sam's great annoyance and disgust, showcasing Dean's love for diner food.

Serving Size: 4 servings

Time: Approximately 45 mins

Ingredients:

For the Fries:

- 4 large russet potatoes, washed and cut into fries

- 2 tbsp vegetable oil

- Salt and black pepper, to taste

For the Chili:

- 1 lb. ground beef

- 1 small onion, finely chopped

- 2 cloves garlic, minced

- 1 can (14 oz.) diced tomatoes

- 1 can (15 oz.) kidney beans, drained and rinsed

- 2 tbsp chili powder

- 1 tsp cumin

- Salt and black pepper, to taste

For the Cheese Sauce:
- 1 cup shredded cheddar cheese

- 1/2 cup milk

- 1 tbsp all-purpose flour

Materials:
- Baking sheets

- Mixing bowls

- Large skillet

- Whisk

- Saucepan

- Serving platter or individual plates

Instructions:
1. Preheat your oven to 425°F (220°C).

2. In a bowl, toss the potato fries with vegetable oil, salt, and black pepper till well coated.

3. Spread the fries in a single layer on a baking

sheet. Bake for about 20-25 mins, until the fries are golden and crispy, flipping them halfway through.

4. In a large skillet over medium-high heat, cook the ground beef till browned and crumbled. Drain any excess fat.

5. Add the chopped onion and garlic to the skillet and cook for a few minutes till the onion is soft.

6. Stir in the diced tomatoes, kidney beans, chili powder, cumin, salt, and black pepper. Simmer for about 10-15 minutes to let the flavors meld.

7. In a small saucepan, heat the milk over medium-low heat till it's warm but not boiling.

8. In a separate bowl, mix the shredded cheddar cheese with flour.

9. Gradually whisk the cheese mixture into the warm milk till it's smooth and well mixed.

10. Arrange the crispy fries on a serving platter or individual plates.

11. Ladle the chili over the fries, and then drizzle the

cheese sauce on top.

Chef's Tips:

- You can customize your chili cheese fries with toppings like diced red onions, jalapeño slices, sour cream, or chopped fresh cilantro.

- For a spicier kick, add a dash of hot sauce or a sprinkle of cayenne pepper to the chili.

- If you prefer, you can use frozen fries instead of making your own from scratch for a quicker preparation.

CHAPTER EIGHT

HEALTH QUAKE SALAD SHAKE (SALAD IN A JAR)

If Dean is known for his love of burgers and apple pie, his little brother Sammy is known for enjoying salads and other healthier food options. Much to Dean's horror, Sam is often seen choosing a salad over a greasy cheeseburger and fries when he gets a chance. One of the most memorable salad moments in the show was during the episode called "Swap Meat," when Sam orders a Health Quake Salad shake. This is where Dean's iconic line, "Oh, you shake it up, baby," comes from.

Serving Size: 1 serving

Time: Approximately 10-15 mins

Ingredients:

For the Salad:

- 2 tbsp vinaigrette dressing (your choice of flavor)

- 1/4 cup cherry tomatoes, halved

- 1/4 cup cucumber, diced

- 1/4 cup bell peppers, diced (use a mix of colors for visual appeal)

- 1/4 cup carrots, thinly sliced or shredded

- 1/4 cup red onion, thinly sliced

- 1/4 cup chickpeas, cooked and drained

- 1/4 cup cooked quinoa or other grains (optional)

- 1 cup fresh mixed greens (e.g., spinach, arugula, or lettuce)

- Pepper and salt, according to taste

For Assembling in the Jar:

- 1 large mason jar with a lid

Materials:

- Cutting board and knife

- Whisk (for mixing dressing)

- A small container for vinaigrette if not using a store-bought dressing

Instructions:

1. If you're making your own vinaigrette, mix the ingredients in a bowl. Whisk together the vinegar, pepper, Dijon mustard, honey, salt, and olive oil until well combined.

2. Start by pouring the vinaigrette dressing into the bottom of the mason jar.

3. Begin layering the solid ingredients in the jar. Add the cherry tomatoes, cucumber, bell peppers, carrots, red

onion, chickpeas, and quinoa (if using). Pack them down slightly to fit more ingredients.

4.   Fill the rest of the jar with mixed greens, packing them down gently.

5.   Seal the jar with the lid, ensuring it's tightly closed. Store the jar in the refrigerator till you're ready to eat.

6.   When you're ready to enjoy your Health Quake Salad Shake, simply give the jar a good shake to distribute the dressing evenly. Pour the contents into a bowl, toss well, and season with additional salt and pepper, if needed.

Chef's Tips:

- Feel free to get creative with your salad ingredients. You can add roasted vegetables, grilled chicken, nuts, seeds, or your favorite salad toppings.

- Make a batch of these salad jars in advance for a quick and convenient meal prep solution. They can stay fresh in the refrigerator for a few days.

- If you prefer a creamier dressing, you can add a small container of dressing separately and pour it over the salad before tossing it.

Chapter Nine

PIG IN A POKE (BREAKFAST SAUSAGE WRAPPED IN PANCAKE)

In the episode titled "Mystery Spot," Sam and Dean go to a local restaurant for breakfast, where Dean orders the Tuesday breakfast special dish called "Pig in a Poke." In this episode, Sam gets stuck in a time loop where he wakes up, and not only is every day Tuesday, but every day Dean dies in a crazy accident! He is forced to live out the same day over and over again, trying to stop Dean's death from happening in various ways. One way that Dean dies is by choking on his breakfast sausage. Pig in a Poke is pretty delicious, but if you're superstitious, you may want to skip eating this dish on a Tuesday.

Serving Size: 4 servings

Time: Approximately 20 mins

Ingredients:

- 8 breakfast sausages (pork or your choice)

- 1 cup all-purpose flour

- 2 tbsp granulated sugar

- 1/2 tsp baking soda

- 1/4 tsp salt

- 1 cup buttermilk

- 1 large egg

- 2 tbsp unsalted butter, melted

- 1 tsp baking powder

- Cooking oil or non-stick cooking spray

- Maple syrup or your preferred pancake topping

Materials:

- Frying pan or griddle

- Mixing bowls

- Skewers or toothpicks

- Spatula

Instructions:

1.　　Heat a frying pan or griddle over medium heat. Cook the breakfast sausages according to the package instructions till they are browned and cooked through. Remove from the pan and set aside.

2.   In a bowl, whisk together the flour, salt, baking powder, baking soda, and sugar.

3.   In another bowl, whisk the buttermilk, egg, and melted butter until well mixed.

4.   Pour the wet ingredients into the dry ingredients and stir till just mixed. Do not overmix; a few lumps are okay.

5.   Insert a skewer or toothpick into each cooked sausage, leaving enough of it exposed to hold onto.

6.   Dip each sausage into the pancake batter, ensuring it's evenly coated. Allow any excess batter to drip off.

7.   Heat the pan or griddle over medium heat and lightly grease it with cooking oil or non-stick cooking spray.

8.   Place the pancake-covered sausages on the hot griddle. Cook till the pancake is golden brown, then flip and cook the other side till it's browned and the pancake is cooked through.

9.   Remove the toothpicks or skewers before serving. Serve your Pig in a Poke with maple syrup or your preferred pancake topping.

Chef's Tips:

- Experiment with different sausage flavors, such as maple, apple, or spicy, to add variety to your Pig in a Poke.

- You can customize your pancake batter by adding a pinch of cinnamon or a handful of chocolate chips for extra flavor.

- If you want to add some savory elements, consider adding shredded cheese, chopped herbs, or even cooked bacon bits to the pancake batter.

CHAPTER TEN

MINI PHILLY CHEESE STEAK SANDWICHES

In the episode "Hollywood Babylon," Sam and Dean go
undercover on a movie set after hearing about a supposed

ghost haunting the production. While they are investigating, Dean thoroughly enjoys the perks of being on a movie set, one of which includes indulging in the catering services. It's here that we see Dean indulging in the delicious and, most importantly, free Mini Philly Cheese Steak Sandwiches. Dean's ability to appreciate the little things in life, like a good meal, serves as a lighthearted contrast to the grimness and horror they usually face on their hunts.

Serving Size: 4 servings (about 8 mini sandwiches)

Time: Approximately 30 mins

Ingredients:

For the Steak:

- 8 slices of thinly shaved steak (sirloin or ribeye)

- 1/2 tsp salt

- 1/4 tsp black pepper

- 1/2 tsp garlic powder

- 1/2 tsp onion powder

- 1/2 cup thinly sliced green bell pepper

- 1/2 cup thinly sliced onion

- 1/2 cup sliced mushrooms (optional)

- 2 tablespoons olive oil

For the Sandwiches:
- 8 mini sandwich rolls or slider buns

- 1 cup shredded provolone cheese

- 2 tbsp mayonnaise

- 2 tbsp Dijon mustard (optional)

- Cooking spray

Materials:
- Skillet or frying pan

- Spatula

- Mixing bowls

- Baking sheet

Instructions:
1. In a mixing bowl, season the shaved steak with salt, black pepper, garlic powder, and onion powder. Toss to coat the meat evenly.

2. Heat a skillet or frying pan over medium-high heat and add 1 tablespoon of olive oil.

3. Sauté the sliced green bell pepper, onion, and mushrooms (if using) in the skillet till they are tender and slightly caramelized, about 5-7 mins. Remove them from the skillet and set them aside.

4. In the same skillet, add the remaining 1 tablespoon of olive oil. Cook the seasoned steak slices for about 1-2 mins on each side till they are browned and cooked to your desired level of doneness. Remove from the skillet.

5. Preheat your oven's broiler.

6. Split the mini sandwich rolls or slider buns in half and arrange them on a baking sheet, cut sides up.

7. Sprinkle a portion of shredded provolone cheese onto the bottom half of each roll.

8. Place the cooked steak slices on top of the cheese.

9. Divide the sautéed peppers, onions, and mushrooms (if using) among the sandwiches.

10. Sprinkle another layer of provolone cheese on top.

11. Place the baking sheet under the broiler for about

1-2 minutes or till the cheese is melted and bubbly.

12. Remove the sandwiches from the oven and assemble the tops of the rolls.

13. In a small bowl, mix the mayonnaise and Dijon mustard (if using). You can spread this mixture on the rolls or serve it on the side for dipping.

Chef's Tips:

- Customize your Mini Philly Cheese Steak Sandwiches with your favorite condiments, such as hot sauce, ketchup, or pickles.

- For a twist, add sliced jalapeños for a spicy kick or top with fresh arugula for a peppery contrast.

- Serve with a side of coleslaw, potato salad, or French fries for a complete meal.

CHAPTER ELEVEN

DEAN'S MINI QUICHES SANDWICHES

In the episode titled "Provenance," Sam and Dean find themselves in New York investigating a mysterious murder of a couple inside a locked house. Their belongings are taken to an auction to be sold, so the boys decide to check it out in case an entity has attached itself to the couple's belongings. While at the auction, Dean naturally gravitates to the food and is seen shoveling mini quiches down his throat.

Serving Size: 12 servings

Time: Approximately 45 mins

Ingredients:

- 12oz thawed pastry pie (follow instructions on packaging)

- 3/8 a cup of milk of your choice

- 2 eggs (or 1 extra large egg)

- 4 diced cherry tomatoes

- 2 slices of ham (optional)

- 3 mushrooms, diced

- 1/2 jalapeno pepper, diced (optional)

- 2 scallions (and an extra 1 for garnish if desired)

- All-purpose flour to dust

- 1/3 cup grated cheese or goat cheese

- oil for greasing

- ½ tsp garlic powder

Materials:
- Mini cupcake baking tray

Instructions:

1. In a bowl, combine the meat, chopped scallions, peppers, spices, cherry tomatoes and mushrooms. In a separate bowl, whisk together your egg(s) and milk. Place them in the refrigerator while you prepare the pastry.

2. Preheat your oven to 425°F (210°C) and lightly grease a mini muffin pan with about 12 spots.

3. Spread some flour on your workstation and unravel the pastry until it is thin enough to use a 3″ circle cutter to make round dough pieces. Place each circle into each cup of the muffin pan, pressing down gently.

4. Fill each cup with an equal amount of the meat and veggie mixture and then pour in the milk and

egg in the bun pits up to 80-90% of the way full. Sprinkle your cheese of choice over each quiche.

5. Bake your quiches for 18-20 minutes or until golden-brown on top and your toothpick comes out of them clean.

6. Feel free to garnish them with another scallion, chopped. Serve them warm with breakfast, lunch, or dinner paired with anything from a salad to a hearty soup, fried mushrooms with avocado on toast, overnight oats, garlic bread, smoothies, muffins, or tea. The options are endless.

Chef's Tips:
- You can trade out the ham for thick-cut bacon, or chicken. Alternatively, you can skip the extra meat altogether and add more chopped veggies instead.

- You can use cheddar cheese, parmesan, goat cheese, etc. There are many cheeses that complement this dish.

CHAPTER TWELVE

JOHN WINCHESTER'S CURE-ALL KITCHEN SINK STEW

In the episode, The Great Escapist, Dean makes Sammy their father's Cure-All Kitchen Sink Stew. He uses "enough cayenne pepper to burn your lips off, just like dad used to make." This meal was clearly not just made to nourish Sam; Dean also wanted Sammy to remember simpler, happier times in their youth. And the normalcy that came from sharing a dish with their father, whom they did not get to spend much quality time with due to the nature of his job.

Serving Size: 6-8 servings

Time: Approximately 2 hours

Ingredients:

- 1/2 lb. each of pork, chicken, beef, and lamb (or your choice of meats), diced into bite-sized pieces

- 2 tbsp olive oil

- 1 onion, chopped

- 2 carrots, sliced

- 2 celery stalks, chopped

- 2 cloves garlic, minced

- 2 cups mixed greens (spinach, lettuce, cabbage), chopped

- 1 cup corn kernels (fresh or frozen)

- 1 cup peas (fresh or frozen)

- 1 red wine bouillon cube (or beef bouillon cube)

- 1/2 cup red wine

- 2 tablespoons Worcestershire sauce

- 1 teaspoon Old Bay Seasoning

- 1 bay leaf

- 2 tablespoons fresh parsley, chopped

- Salt and pepper, to taste

- 1-2 tsps of cayenne pepper (optional but recommended; add more if you like spice, tasting as you go)

- 2 potatoes, diced (optional)

- 4 carrots, sliced and peeled (optional)

- 1 cup pasta, such as elbow macaroni or shells (optional)

Materials:
- Large pot

- Wooden spoon

- Knife and cutting board

- Soup ladle

Instructions:

1.   Heat the olive oil in a large pot over medium-high heat. Add the diced meats and brown them on all sides. Remove the meats and set them aside.

2.   In the same pot, add the chopped onion, carrots, and celery. Sauté for about 5 minutes or till the vegetables start to soften.

3.   Stir in the minced garlic and chopped mixed greens. Sauté for an additional 2 minutes till the greens wilt.

4.   Return the seared meats to the pot and mix them with the sautéed vegetables.

5.   Dissolve the red wine bouillon cube in 4 cups of hot water. Pour it into the pot. Add red wine, Worcestershire sauce, Old Bay Seasoning, and the bay leaf.

6.   Bring the stew to a boil, then reduce the heat to low. Cover and simmer for about 1 hour to allow the flavors to meld. If using potatoes, add them to the stew during this time.

7.   Taste the stew and adjust the seasoning with salt and pepper as needed.

8.   If using corn and peas, add them to the stew. If using pasta, cook it separately according to the package instructions, then add it to the stew.

9.   Just before serving, stir in the fresh parsley.

Chef's Tips:

- This is a flexible recipe that allows you to use up leftover meats and vegetables. Feel free to get creative with what you have on hand.

- Consider serving the stew with a dollop of sour cream, a sprinkle of shredded cheese, or a slice of crusty bread for added flavor and texture.

- You can adjust the thickness of the stew by adding more water or beef broth if desired.

CHAPTER THIRTEEN

DEAN'S FAVORITE MEATLOAF (PIGGLY WIGGLY MEATLOAF)

In the episode titled "Mamma Mia," there is a scene where their mother, Mary Winchester, admits that she never really cooked, contrary to what Dean had believed and nostalgically remembered. She reveals that the meatloaf Dean remembered loving as a child was not actually homemade, but store-bought from the "Piggly Wiggly," a supermarket chain. Store-bought or not, good food is good food.

Serving Size: 6 servings

Time: Approximately 1 hour

Ingredients:

For the Meatloaf:

- 1 1/2 lb. ground beef

- 1/2 lb. ground pork

- 1 small onion, finely chopped

- 2 cloves garlic, minced

- 1/2 cup breadcrumbs

- 1/4 cup milk

- 1/4 cup ketchup

- 2 tbsp Worcestershire sauce

- 2 large eggs

- 1 tsp salt

- 1/2 tsp black pepper

- 1/2 tsp dried thyme

- 1/2 tsp dried oregano

- 1/4 tsp cayenne pepper (adjust to taste)

- 1/4 cup fresh parsley, chopped

For the Glaze:
- 1/4 cup ketchup

- 2 tbsp brown sugar

- 1 tsp Dijon mustard

Materials:

- Mixing bowls

- Baking dish or loaf pan

- Wire rack

- Aluminum foil

Instructions:

1. Preheat your oven to 350°F (175°C).

2. In a large mixing bowl, mix the ground beef, ground pork, chopped onion, minced garlic, breadcrumbs, milk, 1/4 cup ketchup, Worcestershire sauce, eggs, salt, black pepper, thyme, oregano, cayenne pepper, and chopped parsley.

3. Mix the ingredients till well mixed, but avoid overmixing, which can make the meatloaf tough.

4. Shape the mixture into a loaf shape and place it in a baking dish or loaf pan.

5. In a small bowl, whisk together 1/4 cup ketchup, brown sugar, and Dijon mustard.

6. Pour the glaze over the meatloaf, spreading it

evenly to cover the top.

7. Cover the baking dish with aluminum foil and bake in the preheated oven for 45 mins.

8. Remove the foil and continue baking for an additional 15-20 mins, or until the meatloaf is cooked through (internal temperature of 160°F or 71°C) and the top has browned.

9. If desired, broil the meatloaf for a few minutes to caramelize the glaze.

10. Remove the meatloaf from the oven and let it rest for about 10 minutes on a wire rack before slicing.

Chef's Tips:

- Feel free to customize the meatloaf with your favorite seasonings or additional ingredients like bell peppers, shredded cheese, or bacon bits.

- Serve the meatloaf with classic sides like mashed potatoes and green beans, or slice it for sandwiches with extra ketchup or mayo.

- Leftover meatloaf makes delicious sandwiches when placed between two slices of bread or in a bun with some extra glaze.

Chapter Fourteen

Mary's Winchester Surprise Casserole

In the episode titled "Damaged Goods," while paying a visit to Mary at Donna's cabin, Dean asks his mother to make her famous "Winchester Surprise." Interestingly enough, it's the one thing she actually knows how to make. Still, Mary regrets having fed that meal to her husband, John, and Dean, calling it a "heart attack on a plate." Dean isn't phased by this and even requests that she add extra cheese. Dean displays his relatability at this moment, considering most of us have eaten foods from our youth, knowing that they aren't "good for us" just for old times' sake. Enjoy this dish, but, you know, just don't eat it too often.

Serving Size: 8 servings

Time: Approximately 1 hour

Ingredients:

- 1 lb. ground pork

- 1 lb. ground beef

- 1 lb. American cheese, shredded

- 1 cup Fritos (corn chips) for garnish

For the Meatloaf Base:
- 1/2 cup breadcrumbs

- 1/4 cup milk

- 1/4 cup ketchup

- 1 small onion, finely chopped

- 2 cloves garlic, minced

- 1/2 tsp salt

- 1/4 tsp black pepper

For the Creative Add-Ons:
- 1/2 cup bell peppers, diced (red and green for color)

- 1/2 cup canned corn kernels, drained

- 1/2 cup diced tomatoes

- 1/4 cup pickled jalapeños, sliced (adjust to taste for heat)

- 1 tsp chili powder

- 1/2 teaspoon paprika

Materials:

- Large mixing bowl

- Baking dish

- Aluminum foil

Instructions:

1. Preheat your oven to 350°F (175°C).

2. In a large mixing bowl, mix the ground pork, ground beef, breadcrumbs, milk, ketchup, chopped onion, minced garlic, salt, and black pepper. Mix until well mixed.

3. Mix in the diced bell peppers, canned corn, diced tomatoes, pickled jalapeños, chili powder, and paprika. These additions will bring color, flavor, and texture to your meatloaf.

4. Shape the meat mixture into a loaf shape and place it in a baking dish.

5. Cover the baking dish with aluminum foil and bake

in the preheated oven for about 45 minutes.

6.   Remove the foil and sprinkle the shredded American cheese evenly over the meatloaf.

7.   Return the uncovered meatloaf to the oven and bake for an additional 15-20 mins, or until the cheese is melted and bubbly and the meatloaf is cooked through.

8.   Before serving, garnish the meatloaf with crushed Fritos for an added crunch.

Chef's Tips:

- Customize your Mary's Winchester Surprise by incorporating your favorite ingredients or seasonings, such as diced olives, green chilies, or even a drizzle of hot sauce.

- Serve the meatloaf with a side of coleslaw, a salad, or mashed potatoes for a complete meal.

- This recipe is a great way to use up leftovers or include your preferred ingredients in a delicious and creative meatloaf.

CHAPTER FIFTEEN

CAS' BEER-BATTERED TEMPURA TEMPTERS

In the episode titled The Great Escapist, Castiel is on the run from angels and demons, who are after him because he possesses the Angel Tablet. He finds refuge in a remote diner called the Biggerson's Restaurant, where he attempts to hide and blend in with human society. He orders coffee until his waitress, Kara, informs him that to keep the table, he must order more than just the caffeinated beverage. On a whim, Castiel looks through the menu and chooses the Smart-Heart Beer-Battered Tempura Tempters.

Serving Size: 4 servings

Time: Approximately 30 mins

Ingredients:

For the Tempura Tempters:

- 1 lb. medium-sized shrimp, peeled and deveined

- 1 large zucchini, sliced into thin strips

- 1 large sweet potato, peeled and sliced into thin

rounds

- 1 cup all-purpose flour

- 1/2 tsp salt

- 1/4 tsp black pepper

- 1 cup cold beer (your choice of type)

- Cooking oil for frying

For the Dipping Sauce:
- 1/4 cup soy sauce

- 2 tbsp rice vinegar

- 1 tbsp honey

- 1 tsp grated ginger

- 1 clove garlic, minced

- Red pepper flakes (optional, for heat)

Materials:
- Deep fryer or a large, deep saucepan

- Whisk

- Mixing bowls

Instructions:

1. In a small bowl, whisk together the soy sauce, rice vinegar, honey, grated ginger, minced garlic, and red pepper flakes (if using). Set aside.

2. In a large mixing bowl, mix the all-purpose flour, salt, and black pepper.

3. Pour in the cold beer and whisk till you have a smooth and slightly thick batter. It's okay if there are some lumps.

4. Heat the cooking oil in a deep fryer or a large, deep saucepan to 350-375°F (175-190°C).

5. Dip the shrimp, zucchini slices, and sweet potato rounds into the batter, allowing any excess to drip off.

6. Carefully place the battered items into the hot oil and fry till they are golden brown and crispy, which should take about 2-3 mins for the shrimp and 4-5 mins for the vegetables.

7. Use a slotted spoon to remove the tempura

tempters from the oil and place them on a paper towel-lined plate to drain any excess oil.

8. Serve the Cas' Beer-Battered Tempura Tempters with the dipping sauce on the side.

Chef's Tips:

- Be creative with your tempura tempters by adding other vegetables like bell peppers, broccoli, or eggplant.

- For extra flavor, you can sprinkle the tempura with sesame seeds, chopped scallions, or grated lemon zest just before serving.

- Adjust the heat level of the dipping sauce by adding more or fewer red pepper flakes to suit your taste.

CHAPTER SIXTEEN

CAS' PB&J FRENCH TOAST SANDWICH

In the episode entitled "First Born," Cas is seen eating a PB&J sandwich, since he had always loved them as a human - specifically the ones with jelly, not jam. (Jam he found unsettling) As he chews, a grimace comes over his face as he realizes how different food tastes as a non-Earthly being. He describes the taste of his once beloved meal as tasting like "molecules." It's now overwhelming and disgusting. This is a tragic aspect of his humanness that was lost, which is why we dedicate this awesome and delicious version of PB&J to Cas! We kicked this classic sandwich up a notch by making a French Toast version. We know human Cas would be overjoyed! Take a nice, big bite for him.

Serving Size: 2 servings

Time: Approximately 20 mins

Ingredients:

- 4 slices of bread (your choice of type)

- 4 tbsp peanut butter

- 4 tbsp jelly (or the fruit preserves of your choice)

- 2 large eggs

- 1/2 cup milk

- 1/2 tsp vanilla extract

- 1/4 tsp ground cinnamon

- Pinch of salt

- Butter or cooking oil for frying

- Powdered sugar, for dusting

Materials:

- Frying pan or griddle

- Whisk

- Mixing bowl

Instructions:

1.   Take two slices of bread and spread 2 tablespoons of peanut butter on each slice. Then, spread 2 tablespoons of fruit preserves (jelly or jam) on the other two slices of bread. Place the peanut butter and jelly slices together to form two sandwiches.

2.   In a mixing bowl, whisk together the eggs, milk, vanilla extract, ground cinnamon, and a pinch of salt until well combined.

3.   Heat a frying pan or griddle over medium heat and add a small amount of butter or cooking oil to prevent sticking.

4.   Dip each PB&J sandwich into the French toast batter, ensuring both sides are well-coated but not soaked.

5.   Place the dipped sandwiches on the hot griddle. Cook each side until golden brown and the egg mixture is fully cooked, about 2-3 mins per side.

6.   Remove the PB&J French Toast Sandwiches from the griddle and let them cool slightly. Then, dust them with powdered sugar.

Chef's Tips:

- Get creative by using different types of bread for your sandwiches, such as white, whole wheat, or cinnamon swirl for added flavor.

- If you want an extra touch of sweetness, drizzle

the sandwiches with maple syrup or honey before dusting them with powdered sugar.

- Consider adding a few banana slices or fresh berries between the layers of peanut butter and jelly for added texture and flavor.

CHAPTER SEVENTEEN

CAS' PORK RINDS

In the "Supernatural" episode titled "Dark Dynasty," Cas is tasked with guarding Rowena. In a conversation with Rowena and Charlie, he mentions that he grew very fond of pork rinds when he was temporarily human. This comment refers to a period in earlier seasons when Castiel lost his angelic powers and lived as a human. This experience deeply affected Cas, giving him a deeper understanding of and empathy for humanity, reflected in small details like his newfound tastes.

Serving Size: 4 servings

Time: Approximately 30 mins

Ingredients:

- 1 lb. pork skin or pork rind (skin with fat attached)

- 2 tbsp olive oil

- Salt and your choice of seasonings (e.g., paprika, garlic powder, cayenne pepper) to taste

Materials:

- Baking sheet

- Parchment paper or aluminum foil

- Sharp knife or kitchen shears

- Brush for applying oil

Instructions:

1. Preheat your oven to 350°F (175°C).
2. Lay the pork skin flat on a cutting board and use a

sharp knife or kitchen shears to cut it into bite-sized pieces or strips. Make sure to include some fat, as it will become crispy and delicious during baking.

3. Place the pork skin pieces on a baking sheet lined with parchment paper or aluminum foil.

4. Brush the pork skin pieces with olive oil to ensure they become crispy.

5. Sprinkle the pork skin pieces with your choice of seasonings and a pinch of salt. Feel free to get creative with flavors. Some options include paprika for smokiness, garlic powder for extra savory notes, or cayenne pepper for heat.

6. Place the baking sheet in the preheated oven and bake for about 20-25 mins, or until the pork rinds are puffed up, crispy, and golden brown. Keep an eye on them to prevent burning.

7. Remove the pork rinds from the oven and let them cool for a few minutes. They will become even crispier as they cool.

Chef's Tips:

- You can adjust the seasonings to your taste. For variety, consider trying different combinations like BBQ seasoning, smoked paprika, or ranch seasoning.

- Pork rinds are traditionally served as a snack, but

you can also use them as a crunchy topping for salads or as a creative garnish for soups and stews.

- Be cautious while handling hot oil and hot pans when making pork rinds. Use tongs or a spatula to turn and remove them from the oven.

CHAPTER EIGHTEEN

DEAN AND DEATH'S CHICAGO-STYLE PIZZA

In "Two Minutes to Midnight," there is a significant scene where Dean meets with Death, one of the Four Horsemen of the Apocalypse, in a Chicago pizzeria. It turns out that Death handpicked the place for their meeting. When Dean walks in, he finds Death sitting alone in the pizzeria, eating pizza. Death explains that he enjoys the simplicity and flavor of Chicago-style pizza, a small but intriguing insight into his character. This meeting is pivotal to the season's storyline, which centers around the impending apocalypse and the efforts to stop it. It is here that Death reveals he is being forced to participate in the apocalypse against his will. And you know things must be pretty desperate for one of the Horsemen to want to strike a deal with a hunter. Now, you may not be making a deal with Death itself, but there's no reason you, too, can't enjoy a delicious, homemade, Chicago-style pizza pie of your own.

Serving Size: 4 servings

Time: Approximately 2 hours (including dough preparation)

Ingredients:

For the Pizza Dough:

- 2 1/4 tsp active dry yeast

- 1 cup warm water (110°F or 43°C)

- 2 1/2 cups all-purpose flour

- 1/2 cup cornmeal

- 1/4 cup olive oil

- 1 tsp salt

For the Pizza Toppings:

- 1 pound Italian sausage, cooked and crumbled

- 1 1/2 cups shredded mozzarella cheese

- 1/2 cup grated Parmesan cheese

- 1 can (14 ounces) diced tomatoes, drained

- 1/2 tsp dried oregano

- 1/2 tsp dried basil

- 1/2 tsp garlic powder

- 1/2 tsp onion powder

- 1/4 tsp red pepper flakes (adjust to taste)

- Salt and black pepper, to taste

For the Pizza Sauce:

- 1 can (14 ounces) crushed tomatoes

- 1 tsp dried oregano

- 1/2 tsp dried basil

- 1/2 tsp garlic powder

- 1/2 tsp onion powder

- 1/4 tsp sugar

- Salt and black pepper, to taste

Materials:

- 9x13-inch rectangular baking dish or deep-dish pizza pan

- Mixing bowls

- Rolling pin

Instructions:

1. In a small bowl, mix the warm water and active dry yeast. Let it sit for about 5 minutes till it becomes frothy.

2. In a large mixing bowl, mix the flour, cornmeal, olive oil, and salt. Pour in the yeast mixture and

stir till a dough forms.

3. Knead the dough on a floured surface for a few minutes till it's smooth. Place the dough back in the bowl, cover it with a kitchen towel, and let it rise for about 1 hour or till it has doubled in size.

4. In a separate mixing bowl, mix the crushed tomatoes, dried oregano, dried basil, garlic powder, onion powder, sugar, salt, and black pepper to make the pizza sauce. Set it aside.

5. Preheat your oven to 475°F (245°C).

6. Roll out the pizza dough to fit the size of your 9x13-inch baking dish or deep-dish pizza pan.

7. Press the dough into the baking dish, making sure it comes up the sides.

8. Layer the cooked Italian sausage, shredded mozzarella cheese, and grated Parmesan cheese over the dough.

9. Add the drained diced tomatoes and sprinkle them with dried oregano, dried basil, garlic powder, onion powder, red pepper flakes, salt, and

black pepper.

10. Pour the pizza sauce evenly over the toppings.

11. Bake the pizza in the preheated oven for about 25-30 minutes or till the crust is golden-brown and the cheese is bubbly.

Chef's Tips:

- Chicago-style pizza is known for its deep-dish crust and generous layers of toppings, so don't be shy when piling on the ingredients.

- For a personal touch, you can customize your pizza with additional toppings like green peppers, mushrooms, or black olives.

- Let the pizza cool for a few minutes before slicing and serving, as the fillings can be quite hot.

CHAPTER NINETEEN

DEATH'S ENCHILADAS

In the episode titled "Appointment in Samaara," Dean tries to placate Death, one of the Four Horsemen of the Apocalypse, with various Mexican dishes and fried pickle chips, as an offering in exchange for killing him. If there's one thing Dean knows how to do, it's drive a hard bargain. Just a pity his offer did not move Death enough to agree.

Serving Size: 4 servings

Time: Approximately 1 hour

Ingredients:

For the Enchilada Filling:

- 2 cups cooked, shredded, or rotisserie chicken

- 1 small onion, finely chopped

- 1 clove garlic, minced

- 1 can (14 oz.) black beans, drained and rinsed

- 1 can (14 oz.) diced tomatoes with green chilies

- 1 tsp ground cumin

- 1/2 tsp chili powder

- Salt and black pepper, to taste

- 1 cup shredded cheddar or Monterey Jack cheese

For the Enchilada Sauce:

- 2 cans (10 ounces each) of red enchilada sauce (or make your own)

- 1/2 cup sour cream

- 1/2 tsp ground cumin

- 1/2 tsp chili powder

- Salt and black pepper, to taste

For Assembling:
- 8 small flour tortillas

- Chopped fresh cilantro and sliced green onions for garnish

Materials:

- Baking dish

- Skillet

- Mixing bowls

Instructions:

1. In a skillet, sauté the chopped onion and minced garlic in a bit of oil till they become translucent.

2. Add the shredded chicken, black beans, diced tomatoes with green chilies, ground cumin, chili powder, salt, and black pepper. Cook till the mixture is heated through and well mixed.

3. In a separate mixing bowl, mix the red enchilada sauce, sour cream, ground cumin, chili powder, salt, and black pepper to make the enchilada sauce. Mix till it's smooth.

4. Preheat your oven to 350°F (175°C).

5. Spread a small amount of enchilada sauce on the bottom of a baking dish to prevent sticking.

6. Spoon the chicken and black bean mixture into each flour tortilla and roll them up.

7. Place the rolled enchiladas in the baking dish, seam side down.

8. Pour the remaining enchilada sauce over the enchiladas and sprinkle with the shredded cheese.

9. Bake in the preheated oven for about 20-25 mins or until the cheese is melted and bubbly.

10. Garnish the enchiladas with chopped fresh cilantro and sliced green onions before serving.

Chef's Tips:
- You can use ground beef instead of chicken if you prefer.

- You can add diced jalapeños or hot sauce to the chicken and black bean mixture for a spicier kick.

- Serve your Death's Enchiladas with a side of rice and a dollop of sour cream or guacamole.

- Customize your enchiladas with additional toppings like sliced black olives, diced tomatoes, or pickled red onions for extra flavor and texture.

Chapter Twenty

BOBBY'S GINGER PEACH COBBLER

In the episode called "Weekend at Bobby's," his new neighbor knocks on his door and introduces herself. Her name is Marcy Ward, and she offers him her homemade ginger peach cobbler. She has a crush on him and invites him over for dinner and a movie. Bobby hesitates because, like most hunters, he has too much on his plate to entertain a relationship. But when he does try to establish a connection with Marcy after saving her from a demon, Marcy turns him down. It's a huge bummer, but that pie sounded terrific, and now you can try it too! ... And, thankfully, you don't have to worry about an Okami (Japanese demon) waiting to kill you in your room.

Serving Size: 6 servings

Time: Approximately 1 hour

Ingredients:

For the Ginger Peach Filling:

- 6 cups fresh or canned sliced peaches, drained (about 6-8 peaches)

- 1/2 cup granulated sugar

- 1/4 cup brown sugar

- 1 tbsp all-purpose flour

- 1 tsp ground cinnamon

- 1 tsp grated fresh ginger

- Zest and juice of one lemon

For the Cobbler Topping:
- 1 cup all-purpose flour

- 1/4 cup granulated sugar

- 1/4 cup brown sugar

- 1 1/2 tsp baking powder

- 1/2 tsp salt

- 1/2 cup (1 stick) unsalted butter, cold and cut into small cubes

- 1/4 cup boiling water

For Serving:
- Vanilla ice cream or whipped cream (optional)

Materials:
- Baking dish (9x9 inches or similar)

- Mixing bowls

Instructions:

1. Preheat your oven to 375°F (190°C).

2. In a mixing bowl, mix the sliced peaches, granulated sugar, brown sugar, all-purpose flour, ground cinnamon, grated fresh ginger, lemon zest, and lemon juice. Toss till the peaches are well-coated.

3. Transfer the peach mixture into a greased 9x9-inch (or similar size) baking dish.

4. In another mixing bowl, mix the all-purpose flour, granulated sugar, brown sugar, baking powder, and salt.

5. Add the cold, cubed butter to the dry mixture. Using a pastry cutter or your fingers, work the butter into the dry ingredients till the mixture resembles coarse crumbs.

6. Stir in the boiling water till a thick batter forms.

7. Drop spoonfuls of the cobbler topping evenly over the peaches.

8. Bake in the preheated oven for about 40-45 mins,

or till the cobbler topping is golden brown and the peach filling is bubbling.

9. Allow the cobbler to cool slightly before serving. It's excellent on its own, but you can also serve it with a scoop of vanilla ice cream or a dollop of whipped cream for an extra treat.

Chef's Tips:

- You can adjust the amount of ginger to your taste, making it more or less prominent in the filling.

- Feel free to experiment with different fruit combinations or add a handful of fresh berries to the peach filling for a twist.

- The cobbler is best served warm, so you can reheat individual servings in the microwave for about 30 seconds or in the oven for a few minutes.

CHAPTER TWENTY-ONE
"THE ELVIS" BURGER

"The Elvis" Burger is the brain-child of Dean Winchester. Proud of his creation, he shows it to Sammy, claiming that while other versions exist, they're inferior because they take one donut and split it down the middle. Meanwhile, Dean uses two glazed donuts in his versions. When Dean tries to offer it to his little brother, Sam seems horrified and refuses it, stating that he didn't survive hundreds of monster attacks just to get taken out by a double donut monstrosity. Unlike Sammy, we hope you enjoy this superior creation. And remember to finish every bite because there are starving children out there!

Serving Size: 1 burger

Time: Approximately 30 mins

Ingredients:

- 2 Krispy Kreme glazed donuts (original or preferred flavor)

- 1/2 lb. ground beef

- 2 strips of bacon

- 1/2 ripe plantain, peeled and sliced

- Peanut butter (smooth or chunky) for sauce (optional)

- Salt and black pepper, to taste

- Cooking oil for frying

Materials:

- Frying pan

- Grill or stovetop griddle

- Paper towels

Instructions:

1.   In a frying pan over medium heat, cook the bacon till it's crispy. Once done, transfer it to a plate lined with paper towels to drain excess grease.

2.   In the same pan with a bit of bacon grease, fry the sliced plantains till they are golden brown and tender. Remove and set aside.

3.   Season the ground beef with salt and black pepper and shape it into a patty.

4.   Heat a grill or stovetop griddle over medium-high heat. Cook the beef patty to your desired level of doneness (usually about 3-4 mins per side for medium-rare).

5.   Slice each Krispy Kreme donut in half horizontally to create the top and bottom buns.

6.   Spread peanut butter (if using) on the bottom half of the donut bun.

7.   Place the cooked beef patty on top of the peanut butter-covered donut half.

8.   Add the crispy bacon and fried plantain slices on top of the beef patty.

9.   Top with the other half of the Krispy Kreme donut.

10. Serve your Elvis Burger immediately. It's a sweet,

savory, and indulgent treat.

Chef's Tips:

- If you prefer, you can toast the donut halves in a toaster or on the grill for a bit of added texture.

- Experiment with different flavors of Krispy Kreme donuts for a unique twist on The Elvis Burger.

- While peanut butter is a classic Elvis-inspired choice, you can also try other kinds of nut butters, or a drizzle of honey for extra sweetness.

CHAPTER TWENTY-TWO

JACK'S BIRTHDAY CAKE

Jack Kline is a significant character in the final seasons of "Supernatural." He is an incredibly powerful being, as the son of the fallen angel Lucifer. His mother is a human woman named Kelly Kline, which makes him a Nephilim. Jack's birth is initially met with concern and fear due to his immense potential power and his paternal lineage. But, over time, he becomes a key ally and a surrogate family member to Sam, Dean, and Castiel. In the episode called "Jack in the Box," Dean takes the time to bake him a birthday cake. It's far from the most perfect or professional-looking cake, but the love he pours into it showcases Dean's eventual acceptance of Jack as part of the family. Bake this cake for anyone you love and care about, whether they are a blood relative or not. Or, bake it for yourself when your sweet tooth activates, as a small, sweet gesture of self-love and acceptance.

Serving Size: Approximately 12 servings

Time: Approximately 2 hours

Ingredients:

For the Cake:

- 2 1/2 cups all-purpose flour

- 2 1/2 tsp baking powder

- 1/2 tsp baking soda

- 1/2 tsp salt

- 1/2 cup unsalted butter, softened

- 1 1/2 cups granulated sugar

- 3 large eggs

- 2 tsp pure vanilla extract

- 1 1/4 cups whole milk

For the Vanilla Icing:

- 1 cup unsalted butter, softened

- 4 cups confectioners' sugar

- 2 tsp pure vanilla extract

- 3-4 tbsp whole milk

- Optional: Sprinkles and blue icing for writing the name

Materials:
- Two 8-inch round cake pans

- Mixing bowls

- Electric mixer

- Cake decorating tools (if using sprinkles and icing)

Instructions:
1. Preheat your oven to 350°F (175°C). Grease and flour two 8-inch round cake pans.

2. In a mixing bowl, whisk together the flour, baking powder, baking soda, and salt. Set aside.

3. In a separate bowl, use an electric mixer to cream the softened butter and granulated sugar till light and fluffy.

4. Beat in the eggs, one at a time, and then stir in the

vanilla extract.

5. Gradually add the dry ingredients to the wet ingredients, alternating with the milk, beginning and ending with the dry mixture. Stir until just mixed.

6. Divide the cake batter evenly between the prepared pans and smooth the tops.

7. Bake in the preheated oven for 25-30 mins, or till a toothpick inserted into the center comes out clean.

8. Allow the cakes to cool in the pans for about 10 minutes, then remove them from the pans and let them cool completely on wire racks.

For the Vanilla Icing:

1. In a mixing bowl, use an electric mixer to beat the softened butter till creamy and smooth.

2. Gradually add the confectioners' sugar, vanilla extract, and enough milk to reach your desired consistency. Beat until well mixed and smooth.

3. Place one of the cooled cake layers on a serving

platter. Spread a layer of vanilla icing on top.

4. Add the second cake layer on top and cover the entire cake with the remaining vanilla icing.

5. Decorate the cake with sprinkles and write the recipient's name using blue icing (if desired).

Chef's Tips:

Make sure your cake has cooled completely before applying icing, or it will not go on smoothly and may accidentally remove some of the top of your cake!

- Get creative with your cake decorations. To make it extra special, you can use various colors of icing, edible flowers, or themed cake toppers.

- For the best results, make sure your butter is soft, and your ingredients are at room temperature to ensure a smooth cake batter and icing.

- You can customize the cake by adding fillings like fruit preserves, chocolate ganache, or even a layer of fresh berries between the cake layers.

CHAPTER TWENTY-THREE

HIPSTERS' AVOCADO TOAST

In the episode titled "The Foundry," a young couple can

be seen exiting a restaurant, debating how to rate its food on a dining app. While the woman is unimpressed with yet another "avocado toast" joint and wants to give it a two-star rating, her boyfriend counters this sentiment by pointing out that a place serving avocado toast with quail egg is "genius." Thus, he wants to give the place a four-star rating. Now, you can try out the scrumptious avocado toast recipe below, and give it your own rating!

Serving Size: 1 serving

Time: Approximately 10 mins

Ingredients:

- 1 ripe avocado

- 1 slice of your favorite bread (e.g., sourdough, whole-grain, or multigrain)

- 1 quail egg

- Salt and pepper, to taste

- Optional toppings: sliced tomato, crushed red pepper flakes, sliced radishes, microgreens, or crumbled feta cheese

Materials:

- Toaster or oven for toasting the bread

- Frying pan

- Cooking oil (such as olive oil)

- Knife and spoon

Instructions:

1.   Toast the slice of bread in a toaster or oven till it's crispy and golden brown. Set it aside.

2.   Cut the ripe avocado in half, remove the pit, and scoop the flesh into a bowl.

3.   Use a fork to mash the avocado till it reaches your desired level of creaminess. You can leave it slightly chunky or make it perfectly smooth.

4.   Season the mashed avocado with a pinch of salt and a dash of pepper. Mix well.

5.   In a small frying pan, heat a small amount of cooking oil over medium heat. Carefully crack the quail egg into the pan and cook it for about 1-2 mins until the white has set but the yolk remains runny.

6.   Spread the seasoned mashed avocado evenly on the toasted bread.

7.   Carefully place the cooked quail egg on top of the mashed avocado.

8.   Get creative with your toppings. You can sprinkle red pepper flakes for some heat, add sliced radishes for

crunch, garnish with microgreens, or crumble feta cheese over the top.

Chef's Tips:

- You can personalize your Hipsters' Avocado Toast with additional ingredients like smoked salmon, sliced cherry tomatoes, or a drizzle of balsamic glaze for extra flavor.

- Make sure to handle the quail egg gently when cracking it to avoid breaking the yolk.

- Use good-quality bread for the base to ensure a satisfying and hearty avocado toast.

Chapter Twenty-Four

BOBBY'S IRISH COFFEE WITH WHIPPED CREAM

This warm and heady concoction is the perfect post-dinner or nightcap beverage to wine down after a long day of studying lore about supernatural beings, or after a successful hunt. It's also the perfect way to warm up on a cold Winter evening. Its sweetness cuts through its bittersweetness and makes it all the more enjoyable.

Serving Size: 1 serving

Time: Approximately 5 mins

Ingredients:

- 1 cup freshly brewed hot coffee

- 1 1/2 oz (1 shot) Irish whiskey

- 1-2 tsp brown sugar (adjust to taste)

- Freshly whipped cream

- Coffee beans or ground cinnamon for garnish (optional)

- Sweetener to taste (optional)

Materials:

- Coffee maker or kettle

- Coffee mug

- Measuring spoons

- Whipping cream dispenser or hand mixer for whipping cream (optional)

Instructions:

1. Start by brewing a fresh cup of hot coffee. You can use a coffee maker or kettle to prepare your coffee.

2. While the coffee is brewing, choose a heatproof coffee mug. Warm the mug by filling it with hot water and then discard it.

3. Pour the hot coffee into the warmed mug, leaving some space at the top.

4. Stir in 1-2 teaspoons of brown sugar, adjusting the sweetness to your preference. Stir until the sugar is dissolved.

5. Measure 1 1/2 oz (1 shot) of Irish whiskey and pour it into the coffee. Stir to mix.

6. Carefully spoon freshly whipped cream on top of the Irish coffee. The cream should float on the surface of the coffee.

7. For an extra touch, garnish the whipped cream with a coffee bean or a sprinkle of ground cinnamon.

Chef's Tips:

- When whipping the cream, it should be light and airy but not overly stiff. You can use a whipping cream dispenser or a hand mixer for convenience.

- The key to a perfect Irish coffee is freshly brewed hot coffee, good-quality Irish whiskey, and freshly whipped cream.

- You can experiment with the sweetness and adjust the brown sugar to your taste. Some prefer it a bit sweeter, while others like it more balanced.

CHAPTER TWENTY-FIVE

DEATH'S CRONUTS

In the episode "I Think I'm Gonna Like It Here," Dean tells Death that he would have brought him cronuts, if only there were more time. Dean knows that Death would have loved them, considering both share a love of junk food. Shame, really. Oh well, at least you can make your own and enjoy it on Death's behalf.

Serving Size: Approximately 12 cronuts

Time: Approximately 3 hours (including resting time)

Ingredients:

For the Dough:

- 2 1/4 tsp active dry yeast

- 1 cup warm milk (110°F or 43°C)

- 1/4 cup granulated sugar

- 2 1/2 cups all-purpose flour

- 1/4 tsp salt

- 1/4 cup unsalted butter, softened

- 1 large egg

For Frying:

- Vegetable oil, for frying

For the Glaze:

- 1 1/2 cups confectioners' sugar

- 2-3 tbsp milk

- 1 tsp vanilla extract

Materials:

- Mixing bowls

- Rolling pin

- Deep fryer or heavy-bottomed pot

- Slotted spoon

- Paper towels

Instructions:

1. In a small bowl, mix the warm milk and active dry yeast. Let it sit for about 5 minutes till it becomes frothy.

2. In a large mixing bowl, whisk together the granulated sugar, all-purpose flour, and salt.

3. Add the softened butter, yeast mixture, and egg to the dry ingredients. Mix till a dough forms.

4. Knead the dough on a floured surface for a few minutes till it's smooth.

5. Place the dough in a greased bowl, cover it with a kitchen towel, and let it rise for about 1-1.5 hours

or until it has doubled in size.

6. On a floured surface, roll out the dough to about 1/2-inch thickness.

7. Use a round cutter to cut out donut shapes. Then, use a smaller round cutter to remove the center, creating a donut shape.

8. Heat the vegetable oil in a deep fryer or heavy-bottomed pot to 350°F (175°C).

9. Carefully fry the cronuts in batches till they are golden brown, about 1-2 mins per side.

10. Remove the fried cronuts using a slotted spoon and place them on paper towels to drain excess oil.

11. In a mixing bowl, whisk together the confectioners' sugar, milk, and vanilla extract till it forms a smooth glaze.

12. Dip each cronut into the glaze, ensuring they are well-coated.

Chef's Tips:

- Be cautious when working with hot oil, and use a thermometer to monitor the oil temperature for safe frying.

- You can customize your cronuts by adding top-pings like sprinkles, crushed nuts, or flavored glazes.

- Serve the cronuts fresh and warm for the best taste and texture.

CHAPTER TWENTY-SIX

DEATH'S BACON WRAPPED HOTDOG

In the episode titled "Appointment in Samarra," Death invites Dean to sit down at a table and share a meal together. Death has bought himself and Dean hot dogs from "a little stand in Los Angeles known for their bacon dogs." He's already halfway through his own and has saved one for Dean, who hesitates to sit down at the table next to him. Dean has just agreed to spend a day "being Death" in exchange for the real Death to get his brother's soul out of Hell. It's a shame he lost the bet and didn't have the appetite for the food before him. Fortunately, no one in your life needs their soul rescued from Hell, so enjoy this bacon-wrapped hotdog recipe to the fullest extent!

Serving Size: 4 servings

Time: Approximately 30 mins

Ingredients:

- 4 beef or pork hotdogs

- 4 slices of bacon

- 4 hot dog buns

- Condiments and toppings of your choice (ketchup, mustard, mayonnaise, onions, pickles, jalapeños, cheese, etc.)

Materials:

- Frying pan or griddle

- Toothpicks

Instructions:

1.   Take a slice of bacon and wrap it around each hotdog, securing the ends with toothpicks.

2.   Heat a frying pan or griddle over medium heat. Place the bacon-wrapped hotdogs on the hot surface, seam side down. Cook for about 5-7 mins, turning occasionally, till the bacon is crispy and the hotdogs are heated through. Make sure the bacon is evenly cooked on all sides.

3.   While the hotdogs are cooking, you can lightly toast the hot dog buns in the pan or on a separate griddle for a minute or two until they're warm and slightly crisp.

4.   Remove the toothpicks from the bacon-wrapped hotdogs.

5.   Place each bacon-wrapped hotdog in a bun.

6.   Customize your hotdogs with your favorite condiments and toppings. Popular choices include ketchup, mustard, mayonnaise, onions, pickles, jalapeños, and cheese. Feel free to get creative and add anything you like!

Chef's Tips:

- You can use any kind of hotdog you prefer, whether it's beef, pork, turkey, or a vegetarian alternative.

- When wrapping the bacon around the hotdog, you can stretch the bacon slightly to ensure it covers the entire length of the hotdog.

- Be cautious when cooking with toothpicks. Remove them before serving to avoid accidents.

- For an extra twist, you can also melt cheese on top of the hotdogs during the last minute of cooking.

CHAPTER TWENTY-SEVEN

SAM'S APPLE, WALNUT, KALE SALAD

In the episode "The Thing," Sam and Dean are on a quest to gather the ingredients necessary to open a rift to an alternate universe to save their mother and Jack. While they are planning their next move in a diner, Sam opts for a healthier choice, a kale salad, which is a subtle nod to the differences between him and Dean, who often indulges in hearty, comfort food. While a salad may appear to be the smart choice most of the time, Sam's salad ends up being poisoned by Marco Avila, and he is kidnapped.

Serving Size: 4 servings

Time: Approximately 20 mins

Ingredients:

For the Salad:

- 1 cup chopped toasted walnuts

- 1 bunch of fresh kale (about 6-8 cups, stems removed and leaves torn into bite-sized pieces)

- 1/4 cup dried cranberries or raisins

- 2 apples (such as Granny Smith or Honeycrisp), cored and thinly sliced

- 1/2 cup crumbled feta cheese (optional)

- 1/4 cup red onion, thinly sliced

For the Dressing:

- 3 tbsp extra-virgin olive oil

- 1 tsp Dijon mustard

- 2 tbsp apple cider vinegar

- Pepper and salt, according to taste

- 1 tbsp honey

Materials:
- Mixing bowl

- Whisk for dressing

Instructions:

1. In a small bowl, whisk together the extra-virgin olive oil, apple cider vinegar, honey, and Dijon mustard till well mixed.

2. Season the dressing with salt and pepper to taste. Set it aside.

3. Place the torn kale leaves in a large mixing bowl.

4. Drizzle about half of the dressing over the kale. Gently massage the dressing into the kale leaves with your hands for a few minutes. This helps to soften the kale and infuse it with flavor. You'll notice the kale darkening and becoming more

tender.

5. Add the sliced apples, chopped toasted walnuts, crumbled feta cheese (if using), dried cranberries or raisins, and thinly sliced red onion to the bowl with the massaged kale.

6. Drizzle the remaining dressing over the salad.

7. Toss all the ingredients together to ensure they are well mixed and coated with the dressing.

8. Let the salad sit for a few minutes to allow the flavors to meld together.

Chef's Tips:

- For extra protein, you can customize this salad by adding grilled chicken, sliced grilled turkey, or cooked bacon.

- For extra freshness, squeeze some lemon juice over the sliced apples to prevent them from browning.

- This salad can be made ahead of time and stored in the refrigerator. It's even better the next day as the flavors continue to meld.

CHAPTER TWENTY-EIGHT

BOBBY'S JAPANESE STIR FRY

It is not well-known, even amongst die-hard Supernatural fans, that Bobby has a lot of ties to Japan. Bobby once

deciphered a book written entirely in Japanese, impress-
ing Sam with his ability to speak the language as well. In
the episode "Weekend At Bobby's," when he encounters
a Japanese demon - an Okami - Bobby tries to cook a
Japanese dish as an offering to the demon. We learn in
this episode that Bobby visited Japan on a hunting trip
years before Supernatural began. This recipe is a classic
in traditional Japanese cuisine, perfect for you and your
family to savor or offer it up to any pesky Japanese demon.
Enjoy!

Serving Size: 4 servings

Time: Approximately 30 mins

Ingredients:

- 2 cups cooked white rice (preferably cooled or
  day-old rice)

- 1 tbsp mirin (sweet rice wine)

- 2 chicken breasts, thinly sliced

- 1 tbsp sesame oil

- 2 cups broccoli florets

- 1 red bell pepper, thinly sliced

- 2 tbsp vegetable oil for cooking

- 1 yellow bell pepper, thinly sliced

- Pepper and salt, to taste

- 1 carrot, julienned

- 1 cup snap peas, trimmed

- 4 cloves garlic, minced

- 1-inch piece of fresh ginger, minced

- 1/4 cup low-sodium soy sauce

- 2 tbsp oyster sauce

- Sesame seeds and sliced green onions for garnish (optional)

Materials:

- Wok or large skillet

- Mixing bowls

- Chef's knife and cutting board

Instructions:

1.   If you're using freshly cooked rice, allow it to cool. Day-old rice works well for stir-fries.

2.   In a mixing bowl, mix the thinly sliced chicken with the minced garlic and ginger. Season with a pinch of salt and pepper.

3.   In another mixing bowl, whisk together the low-sodium soy sauce, oyster sauce, mirin, and sesame oil. Set the sauce aside.

4.   Heat 1 tablespoon of vegetable oil in a wok or large skillet over high heat.

5.   Add the marinated chicken and stir-fry till it's cooked through and slightly browned. Remove the chicken from the wok and set it aside.

6.   In the same wok, add another tablespoon of vegetable oil.

7.   Add the broccoli, bell peppers, julienned carrot, and snap peas. Stir-fry for a few minutes till the vegetables are tender-crisp.

8.   Return the cooked chicken to the wok with the stir-fried vegetables.

9.   Add the cooked rice to the wok.

10.   Pour the prepared stir-fry sauce over the ingredients in the wok.

11.   Stir and toss everything together, ensuring the sauce evenly coats the chicken, vegetables, and rice. Cook for a few more minutes till everything is heated through.

12.   Optionally, garnish with sesame seeds and sliced

green onions.

Chef's Tips:

- You can customize this stir-fry by adding other vegetables like snow peas, mushrooms, or baby corn.

- To add some heat, consider adding red pepper flakes or Sriracha sauce to the stir-fry sauce.

- Be sure to have all your ingredients prepped and ready to go before starting the stir-fry, as the cooking process is quick.

CHAPTER TWENTY-NINE

DEATH'S PICKLE CHIPS AND DIP

In the episode titled "Appointment in Samaara," Dean tries to placate Death, one of the Four Horsemen of the Apocalypse, with various Mexican dishes and fried pickle chips, as an offering in exchange for killing him. If there's one thing Dean knows how to do, it's drive a hard bargain. Just a pity his offer did not move Death enough to agree.

Serving Size: 4 servings

Time: Approximately 20 mins

Ingredients:

For the Pickle Chips:

- 1 jar of dill pickle chips or spears (about 24 ounces)

- 1 cup all-purpose flour

- 2 large eggs

- 1 1/2 cups panko breadcrumbs

- Vegetable oil, for frying

- Pepper and salt, according to taste

For the Dip:

- 2 tbsp yellow mustard

- 1 cup mayonnaise

- 1 tbsp apple cider vinegar

- 1/2 tsp garlic powder

- 1 tbsp honey

- 1/2 tsp onion powder

Materials:

- Deep fryer or heavy-bottomed pot for frying

- Mixing bowls

- Whisk for the dip

- Paper towels

Instructions:

1. In a mixing bowl, whisk together the mayonnaise, yellow mustard, apple cider vinegar, honey, garlic powder, and onion powder until well combined. This is your pickle dip. Set it aside.

2. Drain the dill pickle chips and pat them dry with paper towels.

3. Set up a breading station with three shallow dishes: one with all-purpose flour, one with beaten eggs, and one with panko breadcrumbs.

4. Dip each pickle chip into the flour, then the beaten eggs, and finally the panko breadcrumbs, ensuring they are well coated at each step.

5. Heat vegetable oil in a deep fryer or heavy-bottomed pot to 350°F (175°C).

6. Carefully add the breaded pickle chips to the hot oil in batches. Fry for about 2-3 minutes until they are golden brown and crispy.

7. Use a slotted spoon to remove the fried pickle chips and place them on paper towels to drain excess oil.

8. Season the fried pickle chips with salt and pepper to taste.

9. Serve the crispy pickle chips with the prepared dip.

Chef's Tips:
- For extra flavor, consider adding a pinch of cayenne pepper to the dip for a hint of heat.

- You can experiment with different types of pickles, such as bread and butter pickles or spicy pickles, to add variety to your pickle chips.

- Serve the pickle chips and dip as an appetizer, game-day snack, or a unique side dish for burgers and sandwiches.

Chapter Thirty

DEATH'S TEX-MEX PLATTER WITH QUESO

In the episode titled "Appointment in Samaara," Dean tries to placate Death, one of the Four Horsemen of the Apocalypse, with various Mexican dishes and fried pickle chips, as an offering in exchange for killing him. If there's one thing Dean knows how to do, it's drive a hard bargain. Just a pity his offer did not move Death enough to agree.

Serving Size: 4 servings

Time: Approximately 30 mins

Ingredients:

For the Queso:

- 1 cup shredded cheddar cheese

- 1/2 tsp chili powder

- 1/2 cup shredded Monterey Jack cheese

- 2 tbsp diced green chilies

- 1/2 cup milk

- 1 tbsp diced jalapeños (adjust to taste)

- 1/2 tsp ground cumin

- Pepper and salt, according to taste

For the Platter:
- Tortilla chips

- Sliced avocado

- Sliced black olives

- Sliced green onions

- Sliced cherry tomatoes

- Sour cream

Materials:
- Small saucepan

- Mixing spoon

- Serving platter or dish

- Bowls for individual ingredients (for serving)

Instructions:

1. In a small saucepan over low heat, mix the shredded cheddar cheese, shredded Monterey Jack cheese, and milk.

2. Stir until the cheeses have melted and the mixture is smooth and creamy.

3. Add the diced green chilies, diced jalapeños, ground cumin, chili powder, salt, and pepper to the cheese mixture. Stir till all the ingredients are well mixed.

4. Keep the queso warm over low heat while you prepare the platter. If it becomes too thick, you can add a little more milk to achieve the desired consistency.

5. Arrange tortilla chips around the edge of a serving platter or dish.

6. In the center of the platter, place a bowl of the prepared queso for dipping.

7. Around the queso, arrange sliced avocado, sliced black olives, sliced green onions, sliced cherry tomatoes, and a bowl of sour cream.

8. Serve the Tex-Mex platter, allowing everyone to dip chips into the queso and customize their chips with various toppings.

Chef's Tips:

- Customize the platter with additional toppings like guacamole, salsa, diced red onions, or chopped cilantro for extra flavor and variety.

- Adjust the heat level of the queso by adding more or fewer jalapeños and chilies according to your preference.

- Keep the queso warm in a small crockpot or fondue pot if you have one to maintain the ideal dipping consistency.

CHAPTER THIRTY-ONE

PEPPERJACK TURDUCKEN SLAMMER

In the episode titled "How To Win Friends And Influence Monsters," in New Jersey, people are turning into a zombie-like state after eating at a local fast-food restaurant called Biggerson's. Dean, Sam, and Bobby decide to investigate the strange occurrences and discover that the restaurant's famous sandwich, the Pepperjack Turducken Slammer sandwich, is laced with a Leviathan food additive. The Leviathans are the season's main antagonists, and they use the sandwich as part of their bigger plan to pacify and eventually consume humanity.

Dean, blissfully unaware of the sandwich's true purpose at first, eats the turducken sandwich and thinks it's delicious. It's only when he begins to feel the effects of the food additive, making him unusually apathetic and lazy, a stark contrast to his usual energetic and passionate demeanor, that it's clear something is very wrong. We've given you a delicious recipe to try it out yourself, but you may want to skip the Leviathan goo.

Serving Size: 1 sandwich

Time: Approximately 15 mins

Ingredients:

- 2 slices of your favorite toasted bread (e.g., white, whole wheat, or sourdough)

- Leviathan goo substitute (ketchup or barbecue sauce)

- 2-3 slices of turducken (pre-cooked or

store-bought)

- Butter or mayonnaise (optional, for spreading)

- 2-3 slices of pepper jack cheese

- 2-3 leaves of fresh lettuce

- 2-3 slices of ripe tomato

Materials:
- Toaster or toaster oven

- Butter knife for spreading (if desired)

- Plate

Instructions:

1.   Toast the slices of bread in a toaster or toaster oven until they are lightly browned and crispy.

2.   If desired, spread a thin layer of butter or mayonnaise on one side of each toasted bread slice.

3.   On one slice of toasted bread, layer the slices of turducken, pepperjack cheese, lettuce, and tomato.

4.   Drizzle your preferred sauce (ketchup or barbecue sauce) over the filling ingredients. This acts as a flavorful alternative to Leviathan goo.

5.   Place the second slice of toasted bread on top,

creating a sandwich.

6.   Use a sharp knife to cut the sandwich in half diagonally or in quarters if desired.

Chef's Tips:

- Turducken is a combination of turkey, duck, and chicken. You can find pre-made turducken slices at some specialty delis or prepare your own if you prefer a homemade version.

- Feel free to customize your Pepperjack Turducken Slammer by adding extras like crispy bacon, avocado slices, or pickles.

- If you'd like to maintain the spicy and gooey element of the original Leviathan goo, you can add a few drops of hot sauce or a spicy chipotle mayo to your sandwich.

CHAPTER THIRTY-TWO

DEAN'S WONDERFUL TAQUITOS

In the episode "Hollywood Babylon," Sam and Dean go
undercover on a movie set after hearing about a supposed

ghost haunting the production. While they are investigating, Dean thoroughly enjoys the perks of being on a movie set, one of which includes indulging in the catering services. It's here that we see Dean indulging in delicious Mini Philly Cheese Steak Sandwiches, as well as taquitos. He offers Sam some, telling him they are "wonderful." And, honestly, we believe him.

Serving Size: 10 servings

Time: Approximately 1 hour and 40 minutes (including prep and baking time)

Ingredients:

For the taquitos:

- 1.25-2 lb beef chuck roast

- 7 oz can of beef broth

- ¼ cup salsa

- 2 ¼ tsp chili powder

- ½ tsp garlic powder

- ¾ tbsp cumin

- ½ tsp dry minced onion powder

- 10 corn tortillas

- Salt and pepper to taste

- Cooking oil for frying

- Toothpicks to assemble

For serving:
- Salsa

- Sour cream

- Shredded cheese

- Thinly sliced iceberg lettuce

- Jalapeno peppers, chopped and seeded

Materials:
- Instant pot

- Non-stick griddle

- Paper towels

- Large skillet

- Toothpicks

Instructions:

Instant Pot Instructions:

1. Start off by seasoning the roast with some salt and pepper. Cut roast into four big pieces before placing them in your instant pot. Next, add your seasonings (garlic, minced onion, chili powder, garlic, cumin, thyme, as well as your salsa and beef broth to form a delicious rub. Then, choose the manual or high-pressure setting for about 50 minutes of cooking time. Once the timer goes off, give the pressure time to release before taking off the lid (approx. 15-20 minutes).

2. Take out the fully cooked chunks of roast from your pot and tear them apart, discarding any large pieces of fat. Put them back in the Instant Pot to stay warm while you prepare them for assembly.

Assembly:

1. If you are frying them, pour 1 ½ inches of your chosen oil into a decent-sized skillet (medium or large) and preheat on medium-high.

2. Drain beef and set aside. Then, turn your stove to medium-high and heat your non-stick griddle over it. Place your tortillas on it and cook for approx. 15 - 30 seconds per side until they become soft and bendable. Take out the tortillas and put

them on a plate that is covered with tinfoil to keep them warm and bendable.

3. Place two tablespoons of the beef mixture into one end of a tortilla, then firmly roll it up. Use a toothpick to ensure the wrap stays closed.

For Fried Taquitos:

1. Make sure that your oil is hot! For instance, your tortillas should be sizzling once they hit the pan.

2. Fry your rolled-up tacos in small quantities so that there is enough space in the pan. You will be frying them for a few short moments on each side, watching and turning them as they cook. Do this until they take on a delicious golden-brown color, and they are crispy all around. Next, put them on a plate lined with paper towels.

For Baked Taquitos:

1. Fire up your oven to 425 degrees F. Misting or lightly brushing oil over the tacos, place them in the oven for 15-20 minutes until they are delightfully crunchy.

2. Serve these tasty treats with your choice of toppings, whether that be lettuce, guacamole, salsa,

sour cream, shredded cheese, jalapeno peppers, etc.

Chef's Tips:

- Feel free to add spices to your mixture that we did not mention here, like cajun spice, Old Bay, dry mustard, smoked paprika, etc. Every adjustment you make is a fun way of experiencing new flavors in your dish.

- Feel free to switch out the beef for pork or chicken instead.

- They freeze well and can be left frozen for up to 3 months while maintaining their taste and quality. Just ensure they have cooled completely before storing them in a freezer-safe container. To defrost, you will need to let them thaw in your fridge overnight, then simply reheat in a hot pan of oil until it is crispy once again.

CHAPTER THIRTY-THREE

GIANT PRETZEL WITH CHEESE

In the episode titled "Monster Movie," the Winchester brothers drive into Pennsylvania to hunt vampires. They stumble across an Oktoberfest that has everything from beer and giant pretzels to live bands and, of course, beautiful barmaids. Naturally drawn to street food and snacks, Dean excitedly shouts, "Oh, big pretzel!" before ordering one for himself and Sam. Good thing you don't need to wait until an Oktoberfest to enjoy this delicious snack yourself!

Serving Size: 4 servings

Time: Approximately 1 hour (including prep and baking time)

Ingredients:

For the Pretzel:

- 1 lb. pizza dough (store-bought or homemade)

- 2/3 cup baking soda

- 1 egg, beaten (for egg wash)

- Coarse sea salt, for sprinkling

For the Cheese Sauce:

- 1 1/2 cups shredded cheddar cheese

- 2 tbsp unsalted butter

- 1/2 cup shredded mozzarella cheese

- 2 tbsp all-purpose flour

- 1 cup milk

- 1/2 tsp Dijon mustard (optional)

- Pepper and salt, according to taste

Materials:
- Large pot

- Baking sheet

- Whisk

- Saucepan

Instructions:
1. Preheat your oven to 425°F (220°C). Line a baking sheet with parchment paper.

2. In a large pot, bring about 6 cups of water to a boil. Once boiling, add the baking soda.

3. While the water is heating, divide the pizza dough into 4 equal portions. Roll each portion into a long rope, about 18 inches in length.

4. Shape each rope into a pretzel shape. You can

form a U-shape, twist the ends around each other, and then press the ends onto the bottom of the U.

5. Carefully dip each pretzel into the boiling water for about 30 seconds. This helps give the pretzels their classic chewy exterior.

6. Place the pretzels on the prepared baking sheet.

7. Brush the tops of the pretzels with the beaten egg and sprinkle with coarse sea salt.

8. Bake in the preheated oven for 12-15 mins, or till the pretzels are golden brown.

9. While the pretzels are baking, prepare the cheese sauce. In a saucepan, melt the butter over medium heat.

10. Stir in the flour to create a roux. Cook for a minute or two, until it starts to turn golden.

11. Gradually whisk in the milk to create a smooth sauce. Cook for a few minutes, stirring constantly till the sauce thickens.

12. Remove the saucepan from heat and stir in the shredded cheddar and mozzarella cheese till

smooth.

13. Add Dijon mustard, salt, and pepper to the cheese sauce if desired. Adjust the seasonings to taste.

14. Once the pretzels are baked and slightly cooled, serve them with the warm cheese sauce for dipping.

Chef's Tips:

- Customize your cheese sauce by adding ingredients like hot sauce, diced jalapeños, or crumbled bacon for extra flavor.

- You can also serve the pretzels with classic mustard or other favorite dipping sauces.

- For a fun twist, try sprinkling the pretzels with sesame seeds, poppy seeds, or everything bagel seasoning before baking.

Chapter Thirty-Four

HEAVEN'S ANGEL CAKE

Okay, okay, so we never really see Castiel eating angel

food cake in the show - and with his sensitivity to human food as an angel, it's no wonder why. But, we felt this recipe was a playful and fitting idea, given his character. Angel cake is a sponge cake known for its light, airy, and fluffy texture. We thought it represented Cas well. That's not to say Castiel isn't brutal and powerful when he needs to be, but in general, he's a pure-hearted being of light. And, if he were to be any cake in the world, we're sure it would be an Angel Cake.

Serving Size: 12 servings

Time: Approximately 2 hours (including baking and cooling time)

Ingredients:

For the Cake:

- 1/4 tsp almond extract (optional)

- 1 1/2 cups egg whites (about 10-12 large eggs)

- 1/4 tsp salt

- 1 1/2 cups granulated sugar

- 1 tsp vanilla extract

- 1 cup cake flour

- 1 1/2 tsp cream of tartar

For the Whipped Cream Topping:
- 2 cups heavy whipping cream

- 1 tsp vanilla extract

- 1/2 cup powdered sugar

- Fresh berries (strawberries, blueberries, raspberries, etc.) for garnish

Materials:
- 10-inch tube pan (angel food cake pan)

- Mixing bowls

- Electric mixer (stand mixer or handheld mixer)

- Sifter

- Cooling rack

Instructions:
1. Preheat your oven to 350°F (175°C).

2. In a mixing bowl, sift together the cake flour and 3/4 cup of granulated sugar. Set this dry mixture aside.

3. In a separate large mixing bowl, beat the egg

whites with an electric mixer on medium speed till they become frothy.

4. Add the cream of tartar, vanilla extract, almond extract (if using), and salt to the egg whites. Continue to beat till soft peaks form.

5. Gradually add the remaining 3/4 cup of granulated sugar, one tablespoon at a time, while continuing to beat. Beat till stiff, glossy peaks form.

6. Gently fold the sifted dry ingredients into the egg white mixture, a little at a time, using a spatula. Be careful not to deflate the egg whites.

7. Spoon the batter into an ungreased 10-inch tube pan (angel food cake pan).

8. Smooth the top and run a knife through the batter to remove any air bubbles.

9. Bake in the preheated oven for 35-40 minutes or till the cake is golden brown and springs back when lightly touched.

10. Invert the pan onto a cooling rack and let the cake cool completely in the pan.

11. In a mixing bowl, whip the heavy whipping cream until it thickens.

12. Gradually add the powdered sugar and vanilla extract while continuing to whip until stiff peaks form.

13. Once the cake is completely cool, run a knife around the edges to release it from the pan.

14. Serve the angel cake with a dollop of whipped cream and fresh berries.

Chef's Tips:

- Angel food cake is delicate, so it's important not to grease the pan to ensure the cake can cling to the sides while baking and rise properly.

- You can use a variety of fresh berries for garnish, and you can also add a drizzle of chocolate sauce or a sprinkle of powdered sugar for extra flair.

- Store any leftover cake in an airtight container to keep it fresh.

CHAPTER THIRTY-FIVE

SERAFINA'S HANGING GARDENS MALIBU SUNSET COCKTAIL

Serafina, an angel who eventually met Adam, and the two became enamored with one another. She kept Adam alive for thousands of years in the gardens, where she served him a specially formulated drink. Together, the couple plotted to kill God. When they meet Dean and Jack, Serafina recounts that she once dreamt about Jack while she and Adam sipped mushroom tea in the Hanging Gardens. This drink is certainly a different take on the ancient drink from the gardens, but it is one that we found very fitting considering all the fresh flavors it has, thanks to the fruits. Consume it in the warmer months for a pleasant and refreshing beverage.

Serving Size: 2 servings

Time: Approx. 5 minutes

Ingredients:

- Ice (enough to fill each glass ¼ of the way)

- 4 oz Malibu Coconut Rum (optional for those who don't drink and can replace it with sparkling water)

- 2 oz Grenadine

- 8 oz Pineapple-orange juice

- Cherries (approx. 2-3 per drink for garnishing)

- Orange slices or pineapple slices (approx. 2-3 per drink for garnishing)

Materials:

- 2 Glasses for drinks

- Ice

Instructions:

1. Start by filling a glass with ice cubes.

2. Gently pour in the rum and the pineapple-orange juice, allowing the liquids to settle.

3. Now, as you tilt the glass, slowly add grenadine until there's an eye-catching, layered effect. Repeat with your second glass.

4. Finally, top the drink off with your cherries and orange slices for a beautiful, picture-worthy finish.

Chef's Tips:

- Serve this cocktail with your favorite appetizer like antipasto skewers, shrimp cocktails, vegetable pinwheels, nuts, crackers and cheese, taquitos, and so much more.

Milton Keynes UK
Ingram Content Group UK Ltd.
UKHW051023220724
445737UK00008B/20

9 781990 841545